LIVING IN... CHINA

by Chloe Perkins
illustrated by Tom Woolley

READY-TO-READ

SIMON SPOTLIGHT

An imprint of Simon & Schuster Children's Publishing Division • New York   London   Toronto   Sydney   New Delhi • 1230 Avenue of the Americas, New York, New York 10020 • This Simon Spotlight edition September 2017 • Text copyright © 2016 by Simon & Schuster, Inc.

GLOSSARY

Coast: land that touches a large body of water

Dumpling: a food that is wrapped in dough and cooked

BCE/CE: how years are measured by the Western calendar; BCE stands for "Before the Common Era" and the year increases as it is further back in time; CE stands for "Common Era" and the year increases as it is further forward in time

Dynasty: a single family or group who rules a country for a long time

Emperor: a person who rules over a country or empire

Invade: to enter and attack a country in a large group without permission

Mongols: a group of people who lived in east-central Asia and ruled China from 1206-1368

Passport book: a small book that says where a person is from and keeps record of the places he or she visits

Peasant: a poor farm worker

Prehistoric: describes a time before history was written down

Rebel: to fight against rules that you do not accept or agree with

Representative: a person who is elected by the people to speak and act for them in government

Republic: a country in which people choose their leaders by voting

Temple: a building used to practice one's religion

NOTE TO READERS: Some of these words may have more than one definition. The definitions above are how these words are used in this book.

Nǐ hǎo! (say: nee how)
That means "hi" in Mandarin Chinese.
My name is Jin,
and I live in China.
China is a country in Asia
where more than
one billion people live . . .
including me!

China is a very big country.
It is the fourth-largest
country in the world!

Because of its size,
China is home to
all sorts of deserts,
mountains, rain forests,
and rivers!

Few people live in
northwestern China.
In the north is the
Gobi Desert, one of the
largest deserts in the world.

In the west are the
Himalayan Mountains.
Many of the highest mountains
on earth are part of
this mountain range,
which crosses through
five countries.

Southern China and its islands are home to rain forests.
The rain forests are filled with animals, such as tigers, monkeys, and elephants!

China's longest rivers, the Yellow and the Yangtze (say: YAHNG-zee), run through central and eastern China. Most people live in eastern China, in cities along the coast.

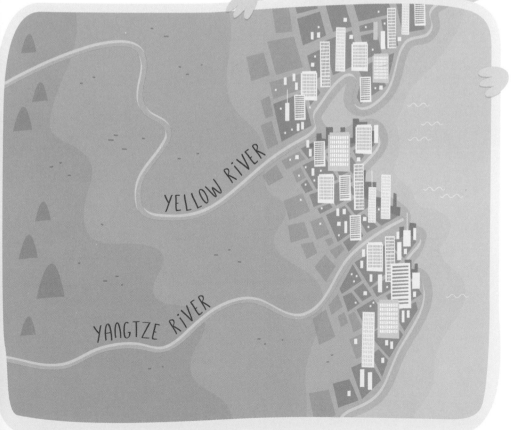

YELLOW RIVER

YANGTZE RIVER

China has some big
cities! Shanghai (say: shang-HI)
is among the biggest cities in
the world: More than twenty-four
million people live there.
Hong Kong is also big.
It has the most skyscrapers
of any city in the world!

Xi'an (say: SEE-ahn) is one of the oldest cities in China. Many cool museums and artifacts from China's history can be found there.

Beijing (say: bay-JING) is our capital. My favorite part of Beijing is the Forbidden City. It is a huge palace where the emperor once lived.

I live in a city in eastern China called Hangzhou (say: HONG-joh). I live with my mom, dad, and aunt Jun in an apartment. Hangzhou is famous for its beautiful lake, Xi Hu (say: SEE-hoo), and many temples.

HANGZHOU

My mom works at a bank, and my dad works for a power company.
Aunt Jun moved in with us last year. She came to find a good job. In China many people move to cities to find better jobs.

Each morning I wake up,
brush my teeth,
and put on my
school uniform.
Then I meet my family
in the kitchen
for breakfast.

Today we are eating noodles with eggs and spring greens. In China we eat most of our food with chopsticks. Have you ever eaten with chopsticks?

After breakfast I take
the public bus to school
with my dad. School
starts at seven thirty, and there
are thirty-five kids in my class.
Our first lesson is
about China's history.

People have been living in
China for at least forty thousand years.
In 221 BCE, Emperor Qin (say: chin)
brought many parts
of China together.
He began building the Great Wall
to protect China from the
Mongol tribes in the north.

In 206 BCE the Han dynasty came to power.
A dynasty is a family that rules a country for a long time, sometimes hundreds of years! During the Han Dynasty there were great improvements in farming.

Over the next one thousand years,
dynasties came and went.
Under the Tang dynasty
China had a great military.
The Song dynasty focused
on art and science.
Then in 1271 the Mongols
invaded China.

One hundred years later
a peasant brought the people
together and overthrew
the Mongols. The peasant
founded the Ming dynasty
and finished building the
Great Wall of China.

China's last ruling
dynasty ended in 1912.
The people rebelled
against the emperor
and created a new
government. Today people
in China vote for
their representatives.

My favorite part of history is learning about all of China's great inventions. The Chinese are credited with inventing paper, printing, silk, and fireworks. A Tang emperor is even said to have made the first ice cream!

After history class we have
math and reading.
Then it's lunchtime!
I'm eating white rice, pork,
and doll cabbage.
Next it's time
for science class.

In science class
we're learning about
animals and plants
from prehistoric
times.

Remember the Gobi Desert?
Eighty million years ago
the Gobi Desert was home
to dinosaurs!
Every year scientists
dig in the desert and find
dinosaur eggs and bones!

Next I have English
and computer class.
On other days of the week
I also have art, music,
and gym class.
School ends at four o'clock,
but today I'm staying late for
extra help on homework.

My dad picks me up,
and we buy *baozi* (say: BOW-zuh)
to eat on the walk
to the bus stop.
Baozi are steamed buns
with different fillings.
Mine has onions, rice,
and pork. Yum!

When we get home, my dad
and I talk about tomorrow.
Tomorrow is the
Dragon Boat Festival!
We celebrate the poet
Qu Yuan (say: choo yoo-AN),
who lived more than
two thousand years ago.

Each year people race dragon boats and eat tasty rice dumplings called *zongzi* (say: ZONG-zuh). I have the day off from school, so my dad and I are going to see the race. I'm so excited!

Aunt Jun and I set the
table for dinner.
My dad made vegetables,
rice, and fish in a
vinegar gravy sauce.
We will also have
soup after dinner.
It looks delicious!

After dinner I get ready
for bed. I flip through
my mom's old
passport book and
look at all the places
she's been. When I grow
up, I want to visit lots of
countries too. Would you like
to visit China someday?

ALL ABOUT
CHINA!

NAME: People's Republic of China (or China for short!)

POPULATION: 1.36 billion

CAPITAL: Beijing

LANGUAGE: Mandarin Chinese is the official language of China. It is written in characters that represent different words. Many Mandarin Chinese speakers can write three to four thousand characters!

TOTAL AREA: 3,705,407 square miles

GOVERNMENT: Communist, Republic

CURRENCY: Yuan

FUN FACT: In many countries you have a first "given" name (such as Sarah) and a last "family" name (such as Smith), but in China your last name is actually your first name! So instead of being called Sarah Smith, people would refer to you as Smith Sarah.

FLAG: Red with a large yellow five-pointed star in the top left corner; to its right are four smaller yellow stars in an arc.